God, Israel, Idolatry and Christ

A Brief Exposition of Isaiah 40 to 57

Hamilton Smith

Scripture Truth Publications

GOD, ISRAEL, IDOLATRY AND CHRIST

Original manuscript dated 1941

FIRST EDITION

FIRST PRINTING September 2018

ISBN: 978-0-901860-98-9 (paperback)

Copyright © 2018 Scripture Truth Publications

A publication of Scripture Truth

All rights reserved. No part of this publication may be reproduced, stored in a retrieval system, or transmitted, in any form or by any means, electronic, mechanical, photocopying, recording or otherwise without prior permission of Scripture Truth Publications.

Scripture quotations, unless otherwise indicated, are taken from The Authorized (King James) Version. Rights in the Authorized Version are vested in the Crown. Reproduced by permission of the Crown's patentee, Cambridge University Press.

Scripture quotations marked "N.Tr." are taken from "The Holy Scriptures, a New Translation from the Original Languages" by J. N. Darby (G Morrish, 1890).

Cover photograph ©iStockphoto.com/iacon (Jeffery Borchert)

Published by Scripture Truth Publications
31-33 Glover Street, Crewe, Cheshire, CW1 3LD

Scripture Truth is an imprint of Central Bible Hammond Trust, a charitable trust

Typesetting by John Rice
Printed and bound by Lightning Source

FOREWORD

The year was 1941 and Hamilton Smith took up a consideration of the later chapters of the prophecy of Isaiah.

What light did the prophecy cast on the events taking place as he wrote? And what did the future hold? Europe was engulfed in war. Jews were suffering unprecedented persecution and they possessed no homeland.

Isaiah's message was a stern one: he conveyed the reasons for God's displeasure with Israel; and yet, beyond all the consequences of failure, the prospect of a regathered nation, safe in the homeland of God's provision, shone through, but only to be enjoyed when the Messiah comes to rule.

In preparing the text for publication some further scripture references have been added because not all today are as familiar with the Bible as Hamilton Smith's generation. The sources of general quotations have been identified where possible, and some contemporary anachronisms have been clarified for today's reader. Otherwise the text has not been changed.

We trust you may be established, edified or encouraged as you read.

John Rice
August 2018

GOD, ISRAEL, IDOLATRY AND CHRIST

CONTENTS

Foreword 3
Isaiah 40 7
Isaiah 41 14
Isaiah 42 18
Isaiah 43 22
Isaiah 44 27
Isaiah 45 30
Isaiah 46 34
Isaiah 47 36
Isaiah 48 39
Isaiah 49 42
Isaiah 50 49
Isaiah 51 to 52:12 54
   Chapter 51 54
   Chapter 52 58
Isaiah 52:13 to 53:12 60
   Chapter 52 60
   Chapter 53 61
Isaiah 54 67
Isaiah 55 69
Isaiah 56 and 57 72
   Chapter 56 72
   Chapter 57 74

GOD, ISRAEL, IDOLATRY AND CHRIST

ISAIAH 40

With the 40th chapter of Isaiah we enter upon the second portion of the prophecy. It falls into two main divisions:–

- First, chapters 40 to 48 in which there comes before us God's controversy with Israel as to their idolatry.

- Secondly, chapters 49 to 57, which bring before us God's controversy with Israel for their greater sin in rejecting Christ.

In the first division of this portion of Isaiah, we find references to idols in every chapter, and this in connection with Israel (see 40:18-25, 41:21-29, 42:17, 43:12, 44:9-20, 45:16, 46:1-7, 47:12-15, 48:5). Thus it becomes evident that the leading subject is God's controversy with Israel as to their idolatry.

In the first eleven verses of chapter 40 we are very blessedly carried beyond the failure of Israel to see that all God's dealings with the Jews will end in the revelation of the glory of the LORD and the blessing of all flesh.

VERSES 1-2

Thus the passage opens with a word of comfort addressed "to the heart of Jerusalem" (N.Tr.). The time is foretold when all her long conflict with her enemies will be forever past; when her iniquities will be pardoned, and all the governmental judgments at the hand of the LORD will have been fulfilled.

Verses 3-5

This time of blessing, however, can only be reached through the intervention of the LORD on behalf of His people. Thus "the way of the LORD" must be prepared that "the glory of the LORD" may be revealed. The world, as we see it today, is but a barren wilderness in which there is nothing to satisfy the heart of God nor meet the need of man. A world in which the lowly are oppressed, the proud exalted, where unrighteousness prevails, and, for the great mass, the circumstances of life are hard. When the glory of the LORD is revealed, His down-trodden people will be delivered, for He will exalt "them of low degree" (Luke 1:52) – "every valley shall be exalted"; all the pride of man will be humbled – "He will put down the mighty from their seats" (Luke 1:52), – "every mountain and hill shall be made low": unrighteousness will be rebuked for "the crooked shall be made straight", and the time of suffering will be ended, for He will feed the hungry with good things (Luke 1:53) and thus make "the rough places a plain" (N.Tr.). The pride and unrighteousness of man are not going to triumph for ever, and the godly will not always be a down-trodden and suffering people. Humility ends in exaltation, and suffering leads to glory.

To prepare the way of the LORD, we know that John the Baptist came as a voice in the wilderness to witness to Jesus. Alas! the nation would neither have John, the witness, nor Jesus, the LORD. As it has been said, "Master and servant were both cut off by wicked hands."[1] Thus, for the time, the revelation of the glory of the LORD to all flesh, and the earthly blessing of man, has been delayed. Nevertheless, the day of glory is surely coming, "for the mouth of the LORD hath spoken".

VERSES 6-8

Seeing that the witness of John is rejected, the frailty of man becomes manifest. Put to the test "all flesh is grass", and any natural "goodliness" that man has is but a flower that fades. This, too, is not only true of the Gentiles – "all flesh", but of the most favoured people – the Jews, for the prophet adds "the people is grass". Nevertheless, though the Jews have lost their kingdom, and the nation has been scattered, and though the Gentiles have utterly failed in government, yet "the word of our God shall stand for ever." Thus, in spite of the failure of Jew and Gentile, faith falls back on the everlasting word of God, and waits for the glory of the LORD to be revealed, and the blessing of man to be secured. One has said, "We may, as only knowing in part, understand but little; but it is a poor feeling, and unworthy to be called faith, only to believe His word when understood."[2]

VERSES 9-11

Thus faith looks on to the time when the good tidings will go forth from Zion, God's earthly centre, and the cry to the cities of Judah will be "Behold your God". When He comes it will be with a "strong hand" to put down the mighty from their seats; with "His arm" He will make the crooked straight, by His "rule" in righteousness. Then He will reward the meek, and all the hard circumstances of

---

[1] W. Kelly, *An Exposition of Isaiah*, Volume 2, Section 5: Isaiah 40 to 48.

[2] W. Kelly, *An Exposition of Isaiah*.

life will be met, for "He shall feed His flock like a shepherd: He shall gather the lambs with His arm, and carry them in His bosom".

VERSES 12-14

Having thus in these introductory verses spoken words of comfort to our hearts and led us to look beyond the long dark night and hail the coming day, as we learn that all God's governmental dealings will end in the revelation of the glory of the LORD and the blessing of man, the prophet passes on to search the consciences of men as to their sin and folly in turning from God to idols. The controversy is opened with a sublime vindication of the majesty of God, Who is the One whose "strong hand" will deal with all the evil and feed His people, whose tender arm will care for the little ones, and "gently lead" the frail and needy.

The waters beneath, the heavens above, and the earth with its mountains and hills, are called to witness that He is none less than the Creator of the universe. The universe, indeed, tells of a God of counsel and judgment, of a God of knowledge and understanding: but who was it directed the Spirit of the LORD? Evidently the wisdom of God is behind the universe, but it is equally manifest that there is no one behind God. In creation God is alone.

VERSES 15-17

Having caught a vision of the Creator, the prophet turns to view the nations in the light of His glory. However great their power and importance in the eyes of man, when seen in the presence of the majesty of God they are but "a drop of a bucket" and "as the small dust of the balance". The isles of the Gentiles are for God only "a very little thing" that He can take up and use at His pleasure. They may defy God and at times oppress His people, but before God they are "as nothing", and indeed counted as less than nothing, for they are vanity.

VERSES 18-25

If then God is so great and man so small, the prophet challenges those who in their folly attempt to make a likeness of the living God. He opens and closes his challenge with the same searching question, "To whom then will ye liken God?" Yet alas! neither riches nor poverty will preserve men from this folly. The rich will set up an idol with gold and silver; the poor will fashion their idol from some enduring wood. But can such plead ignorance? Have they not known? Have they not heard? Has there been no witness of the Creator from the beginning – from the foundations of the earth? Is there no witness to the One before Whom the inhabitants of the earth are mere grasshoppers, and the great ones of the earth are as nothing and vanity, and before Whose power the greatest wither and are taken away like stubble? What folly then to liken God to an image made by the hands of men!

VERSES 26-31

Thus in the presence of the witness of creation to the power and glory of God, Israel is rebuked for their unbelief in turning to idols as if their way, with all its difficulties, was hidden from God and He indifferent to the rights of His people. What folly! The God with whom His people have to do is *everlasting*, and *ever present* as Jehovah – the I AM; He also is the Creator of *the ends* of the earth. There is no place hidden from Him. With Him, too, there is infinite power and unfailing wisdom. He will never faint or grow weary, and who can search to the end of His understanding?

Moreover not only is there infinite power and wisdom with God, but in grace He can give power to His needy people, for "He *giveth* power to the faint: and to them that have no might He increaseth strength". If, however, He giveth strength, we on our side have to learn our need of strength, and that mere natural strength cannot sustain the people of God in the trials they have to meet. Thus we read that the "youths" and the "young men" – those who set forth nature in its freshness and strength – will faint and grow weary and "stumble and fall" (N.Tr.). It is often a hard lesson to learn that the strength of nature cannot keep us in the path of faith.

Further, we learn that if God is the *giver* of strength, and we need strength, it is those who "wait upon the LORD" that are the *receivers* of the strength. Finally we learn the blessed result of being strengthened by the LORD. Such will "mount up with wings as eagles". They will rise above the sorrows of earth to see the glory that is coming. Moreover, they will "run and not be weary; and they shall walk, and not faint".

How rich is the moral instruction of this passage for the people of God in all dispensations as they pass through the trials and sorrows of this world!

- First, there passes before us our unfailing resources in the LORD. He is the everlasting God; He is Jehovah – the ever present I AM; He is the Creator of the ends of the earth, the One with whom there is infinite power and infinite wisdom. He never faints nor wearies, and we never can search to the end of His wisdom.

- Secondly, we learn that God not only has power, but He *gives* power to revive the faint; and strength to those who, in themselves, have no might.

- Thirdly, we are warned that, seeking to walk in our own natural strength, we shall faint, grow weary, and stumble and fall.

- Fourthly, we are instructed that if we are to receive strength it will only be as we "wait upon the LORD". Does not waiting upon the LORD imply prayer, and yet more than prayer. In prayer we make known our needs, in waiting we seek to learn His mind in His presence. In prayer He hears our words; in waiting we sit in His presence and hear His words, like Mary of old who sat at His feet and heard His word.

- Fifthly, this new divinely given strength will enable us to mount up and "seek those things which are above where Christ sitteth on the right hand of God" (Colossians 3:1).

- Sixthly, it will enable us to "run with patience the race that is set before us" (Hebrews 12:1).

- Seventhly, it will enable us, in all the circumstances of life to "walk worthy of the Lord unto all pleasing" (Colossians 1:10) without fainting.

ISAIAH 41

In chapter 40 we have listened to an appeal to the universe as a witness to the glory of God. In this chapter we have fresh witnesses to the glory of God; first by His dealings in judgment with the idolatrous nations (1-7); and secondly, in His dealings in sovereign grace with Israel, bringing the nation into final blessing through a godly remnant (8-20). In the presence of these predictions of judgment and blessing, the vanity of idols is again exposed (21-29).

VERSES 1-7

As ever, God warns before He acts in judgment. So before judgment is carried out upon the idolatrous nations they are invited to "keep silence" and listen to God. We have just heard that "they that wait upon the LORD shall renew their strength" (40:31). Now the "peoples" (N.Tr.) are encouraged to "come near" and "renew their strength".

They are then warned that God has raised up a mighty conqueror from the East to scourge the nations for their idolatry. In a later chapter (45:1) we shall learn that this is Cyrus. Before his irresistible power the nations will be mere stubble. He will pass victoriously into lands where his feet had never before trodden. But behind Cyrus there

ISAIAH 41

will be the directing power of the LORD – the One who knows the whole history of the generations from the beginning. The One who is the first – before all, and will be with the last. Who but the LORD could foretell the coming of Cyrus 200 years before his advent, and thus describe events yet future as if they had already transpired? It will be in vain that the nations, in their fear, will turn to idols, the carpenter and the goldsmith encouraging one another to fashion fresh idols.

VERSES 8-9

In the verses that follow (8-20) we see the glory of God maintained in His dealings in grace with Israel. With the words "But thou, Israel" God turns from the Gentiles to address the Jewish nation. However much they have failed and come under the governmental dealings of God for their idolatry, yet they are the people of God's sovereign choice, the seed of Abraham the friend of God, "called" out from the great ones of the earth, and "chosen" to be God's servant to witness for Him. God may, indeed, chasten His people but He will not cast them off.

VERSE 10

In view of their failure they have come under the judgment of God, but in view of the sovereign choice of God they will, in the end, be blessed. But their blessing depends wholly upon God and His grace. Thus God can say, "I am with thee"; "I am thy God"; "I will strengthen thee"; "I will uphold thee".

VERSES 11-13

Moreover, we are definitely told that all the nations that oppose Israel will ultimately be ashamed, confounded and perish. Those that war against Israel will come to "nothing". Not indeed that Israel has any strength, but because the LORD, Israel's God, will "hold" and "help" Israel.

Verses 14-16

Left to himself Jacob is but a worm and Israel only a "few men" (see KJV margin, N.Tr. note). But Jehovah is the Redeemer and Helper of Israel. Thus, not only will Israel be preserved during the judgment of the nations, but, will become in the hands of the LORD an instrument to carry out His judgment on the nations that have opposed Israel, and to "scatter" those by whom the nation has been scattered. Thus we are carried on to the days when Israel, redeemed from all her enemies, will rejoice in the LORD and glory in the Holy One of Israel.

Verses 17-20

But this godly remnant of the nation – the "few men of Israel" (14), through whom the nation will be restored, is composed of the "poor and needy" – those who find that a world without Christ is but a "wilderness". When in their poverty and need, in their suffering and desolation, they turn to the LORD, He will "hear them". The world may cast them out, but "the God of Israel will not forsake them". He will intervene on their behalf and turn the dry land into springs of water and the wilderness into a garden. In result they will at last see, consider, and understand the ways of the LORD, and then be brought to acknowledge that "the hand of the LORD hath done this".

Verses 21-23

The LORD has foretold the judgment coming upon the idolatrous nations, and the future blessing of restored Israel. In view of these dealings in judgments and grace, the LORD now challenges the Gentiles and their idols. Can their idols foretell what will happen in the future, or show what has happened in the past? Indeed, can they do anything, good or evil?

VERSE 24

God, Himself, answers the challenge. These idols are "less than nothing" (N.Tr.) and their work "nought", and the man that puts his trust in them is an abomination in the sight of the LORD.

VERSE 25

Jehovah has His instrument ready to punish such; one who will come from the North and the East, and calling upon Jehovah's name will trample on the idolatrous nations.

VERSE 26

Who among the idols can declare the end from the beginning? Idols can neither show, nor speak, nor hear.

VERSES 27-29

The One who is the First (compare verse 4) calls upon Zion to behold these idols in all their impotence, and then, in contrast, to remember that Jehovah will give to Zion One that will bring good tidings. Among the idolaters there was no man that could give counsel, or, when challenged, "could answer a word". Their idols are vanity, mere "wind and emptiness" (N.Tr.).

ISAIAH 42

In chapter 41 we have presented the future intervention of God in judgment on the idolatrous nations that have persecuted His earthly people, and the final blessing of Israel. In chapter 42 Christ is presented as the Servant of Jehovah through whom God's righteous judgment and blessing will be carried out.

Verses 1-4

The chapter opens with a touching presentation of Christ as the true Servant of Jehovah – the One who will effectually establish the glory of God on the earth. In contrast to Cyrus who overwhelms the terrified nations with all the pomp of war, this Servant will come in lowly grace. The victorious career of Cyrus may carry out the government of God on idolatry, but he was no delight to God. The moral glory of Christ, in the lowly grace of His perfect Manhood, was a delight to the heart of God.

We know with all certainty that the Servant in this passage is Christ, for the Spirit of God in the gospel of Matthew applies these words to the Lord, at the moment when He refused to take any public place in the nation whose leaders were seeking to destroy Him (Matthew 12:14-21). He would make no national appeal, no standard would

He lift up, and His voice would not be heard in the streets of the city. In such lowly quietness would He pass through the land, that a reed already bruised would not be broken, and a dimly burning flax would not be quenched. This glorious Person who took the form of a Servant, and being found in fashion as a Man humbled Himself, is the One in whom God delights, whom God upholds, and upon whom He puts His Spirit, and through whom, at last, judgment will come to the Gentiles. The mighty ones of the earth have failed and been discouraged in their efforts to bring about universal peace and blessing, but this perfect lowly Man will "not faint nor be in haste" (N.Tr.) until He has set judgment in the earth, and brought the nations to trust in His rule.

VERSES 5-7

Jehovah, the Creator of the heavens and earth, addresses Christ. In chapter 41 Israel is addressed as the servant of Jehovah, and is called and kept (41:8-10). Here Christ takes the place of Israel and is declared to be Jehovah's servant, the One who is called in righteousness, held, and kept to carry out the promises to Israel and bring light to the Gentiles. The blind eyes of the nation will at last be opened to see in the lowly Jesus, that they rejected, the One by whom God will effect their deliverance from the Gentiles and bring them out of darkness into the liberty of grace.

VERSES 8-9

In the light of all that God will do through His lowly Servant, Jehovah appeals to the nation as to their idolatry. They are reminded that their God is Jehovah, the eternal I AM; that His name, and His glory, He will not give to another, nor permit the praise that is due to Him to be given to idols. He alone can bring to pass things already foretold, and declare the things to come before they spring forth.

VERSES 10-12

In view of the blessing that will be secured by the lowly Servant of Jehovah, all the ends of the earth are called to praise Jehovah – to "sing unto the LORD a new song". It is a foretaste of the day when from sea and land, wilderness and city, plain and mountain, praise shall ascend to the glory of the LORD.

VERSES 13-15

This time of universal praise will be reached through the judgment of the nations. The One, who in the beginning of the chapter has been presented in grace as the lowly Man, is now seen in judgment as "a Man of war" prevailing against His enemies. For "long time" God has borne with idolatrous nations, but at last judgment will be executed and their lands laid waste.

VERSES 16-18

Moreover, the judgment of the nations will lead to the deliverance of Israel. As at the Red Sea, Jehovah led His people by a way they had not known and made the darkness light before them, so again the Lord will lead them by a path hitherto untrodden into light and blessing, to the utter shame of those who have trusted in idols. Let the deaf hear and the blind see what God will do for Israel.

VERSES 19-21

If the coming of Christ in power effects deliverance for His people, His coming in humiliation exposed their low moral condition as set forth in these closing verses. Christ is not only the servant of Jehovah, but, as such, He was a messenger to His people. In the perfection of His devotedness He was blind and deaf to all but Jehovah. Seeing many things and with opened ears, yet He never swerved from the path of perfect obedience. Magnifying the law and making it honourable, He was One with whom Jehovah was "well pleased".

VERSES 22-25

But, in contrast to Christ, Israel had not walked in Jehovah's ways, neither were they obedient to His law. Therefore, in the government of God they had become a prey to their enemies. But in spite of all God's dealings Israel had not laid it to heart.

ISAIAH 43

In chapter 42 we have seen Christ presented in all His lowly grace as the Servant of Jehovah, who, in due time, will execute judgment upon evil and bring Israel and the nations into blessing.

In the 43rd chapter we learn that sovereign grace having established Israel in blessing (1-7), will make them a witness to the one true God before the nations, to show forth His praise (8-21). At the same time we learn that God is not indifferent to the sins of His people that in grace will be blotted out (22-28).

Verses 1-2

From the close of the last chapter we learn that Israel had not only broken the law and rebelled against Jehovah, but, when chastened, "he laid it not to heart" (42:25). How low must be the moral condition of God's people when they are untouched by the discipline of the Lord! But will God, therefore, give up His people? Ah no! The coming of Christ as the perfect Servant enables God to fall back on His sovereignty and use the very evil of His people for an occasion to display His grace. Thus, in spite of all their failure the Lord can say to Israel, "Fear not" (1, 5). On the ground of their sad history in relation to God they had everything to fear; but now God will act toward them on the ground of what He has done for them in grace. Thus He can say, "I have redeemed thee, I have called thee by thy name; thou art Mine". Because of their own failure they may have to pass through the cleansing waters and the purifying fire, but the LORD can say, "I will be with thee". If the Lord is with His people in all their trials we may be sure they will be brought "*through*". They may be "tried with fire", and pass through "the fiery trial" (1 Peter 1:7, 4:12) but they will neither be overwhelmed by the flood nor destroyed by the fire. Of old, in a literal sense, Israel had to face the waters of the Red Sea, and Daniel the fiery furnace, but the Son of God was with him in the furnace and brought him through the fire (Daniel 3:2).

VERSE 3

But if Israel is brought through the trial into final blessing it is not because of any merit in Israel, but wholly on the ground of Who God is, "For", says God, "I am the LORD thy God, the Holy One of Israel, thy Saviour". Israel must endure the fire and the water, for God is "the Holy One", but they will be brought through, for God is their Saviour.

VERSES 4-7

In the past, Egypt, Ethiopia and Seba, were given over to judgment to ransom God's people from their power. So in the future, the nations that have persecuted Israel will be given up to judgment, for, in God's sight, His people are "precious" and "honourable", and "loved" by God. Therefore, in spite of all failure on their part, God is with them, and will gather them back to their land from the ends of the earth. They are called by God's name, and are created for His glory. Thus, in bringing Israel into final blessing, God is acting for the glory of His great name.

VERSES 8-9

God's sovereign intervention on behalf of Israel having been foretold, an appeal is made to the nations that they may be brought to acknowledge the true God through His ways with Israel. Israel, who with their eyes had seen the glory of Jehovah, and heard His law, had blindly turned to idols and had been deaf to the warnings of the prophets. Nevertheless in their restoration they will become a witness to the one true God.

All the nations are warned to heed God's declaration concerning the future of Israel. The nations may gather together and assemble in conferences, in their effort to govern the world, but they cannot show the former things, and still less the things to come. Let them hear and confess that this is the truth.

VERSES 10-11

Israel is the standing witness to the world that God is the One God that men "may know and believe" that God is the eternal One – none before, and no one after, the "I AM", and the only Saviour.

VERSES 12-13

In reference to Israel, God can say, "I have *declared* and have *saved* and I have *showed*". Before they turned to idols, God had already declared the past and the future as to Israel, and speaking as the I AM, to Whom the future is present, He can say "I have saved". Having saved, God can say to all the world that Israel are "My witnesses … that I am God". God is the God of eternity. Before time was – "before the day" – God can say I AM; and God is omnipotent, for none can deliver out of His hand or hinder His work.

ISAIAH 43

VERSES 14-17

Turning from the nations to Israel, God encourages His people by saying, I am "your Redeemer", "your Holy One", "your King". For Israel's sake God had humbled the pride of Babylon, the centre of idolatry, as in the past He had made a way for His people through the sea and overthrown the host of the Egyptians.

VERSES 18-21

Let Israel remember and consider God's deliverances in the past, and thus trust God for the "new thing" about to take place in the future. In the past God made "a way in the sea" (16); in the future He will make "a way in the wilderness" for His people to return to their land. He will refresh and sustain them on their journey with rivers in the deserts, and protect them from "the beast of the field". Thus, at last, they will "show forth" Jehovah's praise and thus fulfil the purpose for which they were formed.

VERSES 22-25

But if the LORD deals in sovereign grace with His people, and will yet use them as a witness to the nations, it is not that He is indifferent to their failure. Thus, basing His appeal upon all that He is, and will yet do in sovereign grace, He rebukes them for their low condition. In their distress they had not called upon the LORD, and when settled in the land they had grown weary of the LORD. Instead of bringing to Jehovah the sacrifices which speak of Christ to God, they had made God toil in governmental dealings with them, and wearied Him with their sins. They were weary of God, and God, to use the language of men, was wearied with their evil ways (22, 24). Nevertheless, for His own sake, God will blot out their transgressions and remember their sins no more.

Verses 26-28

But before God can righteously remember their sins no more, He must be put in remembrance. In other words, there must be the fullest confession on the part of Israel of their sins, before God can justify. So Jehovah has to say; "Put Me in remembrance: let us plead together: *declare* thou, that thou mayest be justified". Let Israel go back to their "first father" and confess the sin and rebellion against Jehovah, and that therefore God has "profaned the princes of the sanctuary", "given Jacob to the ban" (N.Tr.), "and Israel to reproaches". When Israel thus confesses their sin and justifies God in His dealings with them, God will justify Israel, blot out their transgressions and remember their sin no more.

ISAIAH 44

We have seen that in sovereign grace Israel will be brought into final blessing, but that this in no wise means that God is indifferent to the sins of the nation. Now we are to learn that in the midst of all the failure of the nation there is a preserved remnant through whom this sovereign grace of God will bring the nation into blessing (1-8); that the idolaters will become a witness to the vanity of their idols (9-20); but in spite of the failure of man, Jehovah will glorify Himself in Israel and use the Gentiles to perform His pleasure (21-28).

Verses 1-5

However great the failure of Israel and their princes, bringing them under the curse and reproaches (43:28), yet the sovereign choice of God remains that will bring the nation into blessing through a godly remnant, "For", says the LORD, "I will pour water upon *him* that is thirsty, and floods upon the dry ground". Thus the LORD will revive those in Israel who are conscious of their need and deplore their condition. From this remnant will come a seed, and an offspring, through whom the LORD will establish the nation in blessing. Instead of being as one thirsty in a parched land, they will be like willows planted by the water courses. In that day each will gladly own the LORD, and, without shame or reproach, confess to being an Israelite.

Verses 6-8

Restored Israel will be used as a witness to Jehovah, the King of Israel, by whom the nation has been redeemed from the power of the enemy. They will witness that God is the first and the last – the One who is before all and will remain though men pass away. He alone can declare the things to come. If there are those who think otherwise, let them declare to Israel the things to come. But Israel need not fear, for they are God's witness that there is no other God but Jehovah.

Verses 9-17

But if Israel witnesses to God, the idolaters become their own witness to the vanity of their idols. They that make the idols are "all of them vanity", and their images "profitable for nothing". They "see not, nor know", and their impotence brings shame to their makers. The smith of his own strength fashions a metal god, and the carpenter a wooden idol "after the figure of a man". To this end he cuts down the trees of the forest; with part of the wood he makes a fire to warm himself, with part he bakes his bread, and with part he makes a graven image before which he bows down and worships.

Verses 18-20

The terrible effect of such folly is to darken the understanding and harden the heart. Deceived by the imaginations of their own heart, they cannot discern the lie, nor deliver their souls from its effect.

ISAIAH 44

Verses 21-23

Israel is called to remember that, in contrast to these idolaters who form their own gods, Jehovah has formed His people to serve Him. Having formed them He will not forget them: He will blot out their sins, redeem them from the power of the enemy, and glorify Himself in Israel. In result the heavens and the earth will join to sing His praise.

Verses 24-28

But if the Lord is the Redeemer of Israel, He is also the Creator of the heavens and the earth and can, and will, dispose of all men according to His pleasure. He brings to nothing the deceptions of idolaters, but confirms the word of His messengers. He will build again Jerusalem and the cities of Judah, will dry up the rivers and remove every hindrance to the return of His people, and use a Gentile king to perform His pleasure.

ISAIAH 45

The 44th chapter closes with a reference to Cyrus, the Gentile king that God was going to use for the rebuilding of Jerusalem. In the 45th chapter we learn that through this king the governmental judgment of God would fall upon the idolatrous nations (1-10); and His people be set free from captivity (11-13). Moreover, this deliverance would foreshadow the future "everlasting salvation" of Israel (14-19), and the final universal submission of the nations to Jehovah (20-25).

Verses 1-3

The Lord foretells the victorious career of Cyrus, the Persian king, the instrument that God was going to use to subdue the nations that had persecuted His people. This judgment would specially fall upon Babylon, the first great world empire during the times of the Gentiles, that had held the people of God in captivity. Under the siege of Babylon the brazen gates of the city would be broken in pieces, and the bars of iron cut asunder. The loins of kings would be loosed in terror, and their hidden riches discovered (Daniel 5:6, Nahum 2:6).

ISAIAH 45

VERSES 4-5

It is, however, for the sake of Israel, God's elect, that Cyrus is called, and allowed to subdue the nations, little as Cyrus may imagine that he is an instrument in the hands of God. Two hundred years before he comes upon the scene God can say, "I have even *called thee* by thy name: I have *surnamed thee*", and "I *girded thee*, though thou hast not known Me".

VERSES 6-8

In raising up Cyrus, God would have all nations know that He is God and there is none else beside. The truth as to Jehovah is presented in contrast to the Zoroastrian belief of the Persians, by which they held that a certain eternal person brought into existence two powerful beings; one the creator of all good, and the other the author of all evils that afflict men. It is God who forms the light and creates the darkness; it is God who makes peace among the nations, and, in His governmental ways creates evil in the sense of punishment (see Job 2:10, Jeremiah 18:7-10). It is the LORD that does these things with the final result that blessing will descend from heaven, which earth will be open to receive. It will not be righteousness without grace, nor salvation at the expense of righteousness, but salvation and righteousness will "spring up together".

VERSES 9-10

In view of the judgments coming upon idolatry, God warns the idolaters. In turning from God to idols man is striving with his Maker. Let created men – mere potsherds – strive together, but woe unto them if they call God's works, and God's ways, in question.

VERSES 11-13

If, however, God warns those who turn to idols, He encourages Israel to enquire of Himself concerning those in relationship with Himself, and as to His work on their behalf. The God who created the earth and its inhabitants, and the heavens with all their host, is the One who alone can foretell their destiny. God, too, can "direct" man's ways, and use men to carry out His purposes. Thus God raises up Cyrus, and "will direct all his ways" for the fulfilment of His purpose to rebuild Jerusalem and set free His captive people.

VERSES 14-19

The judgment of Babylon, and the partial deliverance of God's people under Cyrus is, however, only a foreshadowing of the universal judgment of the nations and the regathering of Israel under the reign of Christ. Thus, passing on to the last days, the Spirit of God through the prophet foretells how those who had held Israel in bondage will themselves become subject to Israel. In the past Israel had made supplication to their Egyptian tormentors, but the time is yet to come when Egypt will supplicate Israel for mercy and, instead of saying as in the days of old, "Who is the LORD"? (Exodus 5:2), they will confess, "Surely God is in thee, and there is none else, no other God" (N.Tr.). God, in His governmental dealings with the nation, may for a season hide Himself; but, nevertheless, He is the "God of Israel, the Saviour" who is disposing of all men and events for the display of His own glory in bringing to shame and confusion the idolatrous nations, and blessing His people Israel with "an everlasting salvation" from their enemies and the shame by which for long centuries they have been overshadowed.

ISAIAH 45

VERSES 20-25

Moreover, if there is future blessing for Israel through a godly remnant, so there is blessing for the "escaped of the nations" – those who are brought through God's earthly judgments.

In view of this blessing:–

- First, the prophet exposes the ignorance and folly of those who set up a graven image and pray to a god that cannot save.

- Secondly, God is presented as the only God – "A just God and a Saviour" – One who deals in righteousness with sins, and yet can save the sinner.

- Thirdly, seeing the folly and evil of idolatry, and the blessedness of the true God, an appeal is made to all the ends of the earth to look to God and be saved.

- Fourthly, if men will not look to God and be saved, they are warned that the time is coming when, through judgment, they will be compelled to own the rights of God. The word has gone forth from God's mouth in righteousness, and will not be recalled, "That unto Me every knee shall bow, and every tongue shall swear".

- Finally, we are told the result of this appeal. One the one hand, there will be those who will come to God confessing that, "only" (N.Tr.) "in the LORD" they have "righteousness and strength". On the other hand, there will be alas! those who are incensed against God and will come to shame. Israel will, at last, be found amongst those who confess that "in the LORD" they are justified, and thus glory in Him.

ISAIAH 46

In the opening verses of chapter 46 we have the futility of idols contrasted with the might of Jehovah.

VERSES 1-2

Bel and Nebo, the helpless gods of Babylon, have to be borne as a heavy burden on weary beasts who cannot deliver them from being captured by Cyrus, the Persian king.

VERSES 3-4

In contrast to these helpless idols, that have to be carried, the house of Israel is reminded that Jehovah carries the remnant of Israel. Moreover, while His people may change and grow old, there is no change with God, for He can say, "'even to your old age I am He" (literally, "I, the SAME"). He made His people, carries them, and will deliver them from all their enemies.

VERSES 5-7

Idols are thus contrasted with Jehovah, but cannot for one moment be compared with the true God. Jehovah is the Maker, but an idol has to be made, and, when made, instead of bearing others has to be borne; and when set in his place is unable to move, cannot respond to the cry of need, nor save from trouble.

Verses 8-11

The transgressors – those in Israel who had turned aside to idols – are called to remember these things and show themselves men. Let them remember the former actings of God and acknowledge that there is no other God but Jehovah, and none like God, Who declares the end from the beginning and brings to pass His counsels, fulfilling His plans. Thus God sees fit to use "a ravenous bird", like Cyrus, to execute judgment upon idolatry, proving that what God has said He will bring to pass, and what God has purposed He will do.

Verses 12-13

In view of coming judgment the stout-hearted idolaters of Babylon, who are far from righteousness, are warned that God is about to bring near His righteousness. The result will be judgment on the stout-hearted who resist God; salvation for His people, and glory for His own great Name.

ISAIAH 47

In the 46th chapter we have learned the folly of idols, in this chapter we have the exposure of the nakedness and shame of those who turn from God to idols and spiritual wickedness.

VERSES 1-3

The destruction of Babylon is foretold. The empire would be laid in the dust. Instead of living delicately, the Chaldeans would, with shame, pass over the river into captivity. From ruling over the world as the mistress of kingdoms, the first great Gentile empire would fall into the condition of a slave at the millstone. Thus God would take vengeance on those who had shown no mercy to His people, and none would stay His hand (N.Tr.).

VERSES 4-5

But, says the prophet, the One who is going to take vengeance on Babylon is "Our Redeemer, the LORD of hosts … the Holy One of Israel". It follows that the judgment of Babylon and all that this city represents, will be the deliverance of Israel. The Jew will thus come into the light of God's favour, while the Gentile, that had ruled the nations, would pass into silence and darkness; thus proving how true are the words of Hannah's song. "He will keep the feet of His saints, and the wicked shall be silent in darkness" (1 Samuel 2:9).

Verse 6

Further, Babylon is clearly told why judgment overtakes this world empire.

First, this Gentile power had shown *"no mercy" to God's people*, when, in His governmental dealings, they had been delivered into the hand of Babylon.

Verse 7

Secondly, the Gentile power had been *heedless of every warning* as to their sins and the coming judgment. They had not laid these things to heart, nor considered their "latter end".

Verse 8

Thirdly, the Gentile power had given itself over to *self-indulgence*, seeking only the pleasures of the world, living carelessly without consideration for any but themselves.

Fourthly, the Gentile power was marked by *self-confidence* which deceived them into saying that they would never be left desolate or suffer any loss.

Verses 9-11

Fifthly, they had turned to *spiritual wickedness* putting their trust in "sorceries" and "enchantments".

Sixthly, the Gentile power had *thrown off all fear of God*, for it said, "None seeth me", and in the heart it was said, "It is I, and there is none beside me".

How solemn, as we look upon the world of our day, to see in corrupt Christendom a spiritual Babylon which bears all the marks of the historical Babylon as set forth, by the

Spirit of God, for our warning, in the 18th chapter of Revelation.

VERSES 12-13

The overthrow of Babylon exposes the absolute worthlessness of sorceries and enchantments. If there is any profit in sorcery let Babylon turn to the multitude of her sorceries and enchantments, if so be that she may prevail against her enemies. Let the astrologers and stargazers, and those who predict according to the new moons, stand up and save Babylon.

VERSES 14-15

But, says God, they cannot deliver themselves from judgment, much less Babylon. Her merchants, with all their wealth cannot save Babylon. When God's judgment falls "none shall save".

ISAIAH 48

The 48th chapter records the final appeal of Jehovah to Israel as to their sin in turning aside to idols, with the assurance that God will yet deliver them from the captivity to the Gentiles, into which their sin has brought them, for His name's sake (9).

VERSES 1-2

The appeal is to those of Judah who profess the Name of the LORD, and boast in "the holy City", but "not in truth, nor in righteousness".

VERSES 3-5

Knowing the obstinacy and perverseness of the nation, God had, in the past, foretold future events, which in due time had suddenly come to pass. Thus they had no possible ground for pretending that their idols had forewarned them.

VERSES 6-8

Moreover, if they will not own that this is so, let them consider the "new things" that Jehovah will show from the present time. Things as yet hidden and unknown. Of such things not one could say, "Behold I knew them".

Knowing the treachery of their hearts, God leaves them without excuse.

VERSES 9-11

Then we learn why God had not cut them off. For His own name's sake, and for His praise, Jehovah had spared them. Nevertheless, for His own sake God had also chastened them in passing them through "the furnace of affliction".

VERSES 12-16

Having reminded them of their sin, and God's dealings in chastening, an appeal is now made to Israel – the nation that God had called from the Gentiles. Let them remember that Jehovah is the first and the last, the Creator of the earth and the heavens. Let them assemble together and hear the new things that God foretells. The LORD had called Cyrus, one who will carry out God's pleasure on Babylon, and whose arm of might will fall upon the Chaldeans. Under the providence of God, his way will prosper. Now, says the prophet, let the nations come near and hear things that are not spoken in secret but in public by one sent from the Lord GOD in the power of the Spirit.

VERSES 17-19

This portion of the prophecy closes with a touching appeal in which the LORD reminds Israel that He is their Redeemer; having redeemed them, He is their Teacher to instruct them in His mind, and having instructed them, He is their Leader to take them in the way that they should go – the way of blessing for themselves and of glory to God. In principle God takes the same way with His people today. Had the people of God in that day, and in this, listened to the teaching and followed the One that

ISAIAH 48

leads, how great would have been their blessing, and what sorrows they would have been saved.

Verses 20-21

Nevertheless the Spirit of God foretells the time when the nation will go forth from the captivity of Babylon, the foreshadowing of the yet greater deliverance from the Gentiles in a future day, when restored Israel will be a witness "to the end of the earth" that the LORD has redeemed them, and, as of old, has led them through the wilderness into blessing.

Verse 22

The prophecy closes with the warning that, whatever blessing is reserved for God's people, it remains true that there is no peace for the wicked. Let the Gentiles, who, throughout the ages, have taken advantage of the chastening hand of God upon the Jews to ruthlessly persecute them, take heed to the warning.

ISAIAH 49

In the division of the Book of the prophet Isaiah extending from chapter 49 to the end of chapter 57, we have foretold the transcendent event of the coming into the world of the Lord Jesus as the Servant of Jehovah. We learn moreover, that through His coming into the world the evil of man's heart is exposed in all its terrible extent inasmuch as Christ is rejected and crucified. Nevertheless, if the sin of man is exposed, we see also that Jesus, as the Servant of Jehovah, brings into display, and carries into effect, the will of God. Thus it is foretold that in the end, God's glory will be secured, His counsels fulfilled, Christ will be glorified, the wicked will be overthrown, the godly brought into blessing, and the heavens and the earth will join in praise to God.

Moreover, in this great passage we learn that the final blessing can only be reached by the Servant of Jehovah becoming obedient unto death. The atoning sufferings must come before the displayed glory.

The passage opens with a striking summary, in the first thirteen verses, of the results that follow from Christ taking the place, in this world, of the Servant of Jehovah.

ISAIAH 49

Verse 1

In the first four verses we hear the voice of Christ through the Spirit of prophecy. The Lord calls upon the Isles of the Gentiles, and the nations from afar, to listen to His words. All are to know that He is "called" by Jehovah, and His Name announced before His birth. In blessed fulfilment of these words, we read in the Gospel of Matthew, of the Angel announcing to Joseph, concerning Mary, that "she shall bring forth a son, and thou shalt call His name JESUS". All the nations are to know that JESUS, the Servant of Jehovah, is the Saviour of the world.

Verse 2

Moreover, the One who is the Saviour will also convict us of our sins, and thus manifest our need of the Saviour. His word will be like a sharp sword, and a polished shaft, piercing the conscience, and revealing the thoughts and intents of the heart (Luke 2:35).

Verse 3

Further, the Saviour of the world is the Servant of Jehovah to carry out the will of God. Even as Jesus is the true Vine in the place of Israel the degenerate vine (Jeremiah 2:21), so Jesus becomes the true Servant in the place of the nation that had entirely failed as the servant of Jehovah. Thus, it would seem, that Christ is addressed when Jehovah says, "Thou are my Servant, O Israel".

In the portion that follows we have very blessedly foretold the results of Jesus becoming the Servant of Jehovah. First, and above all else, if Christ takes the place of the Servant, He will be the One of whom God can say "I will be glorified". Thus at His birth the heavenly host can say, "Glory to God in the highest" (Luke 2:14), and at the end of His path, in anticipation of the Cross, the Lord can say,

"Now is the Son of Man glorified, and God is glorified in Him" (John 13:31). Men had dishonoured God, but at last when Jesus became Man, there was One in Whom God was glorified.

VERSE 4

Secondly, it is foretold that the One in Whom God will be glorified will be rejected of Israel. As the Servant, Christ laboured in the midst of Israel. But He has to say, "I have laboured in vain, I have spent My strength for nought, and in vain". So in the gospel day we hear the Lord "upbraid the cities wherein most of His mighty works were done, because they repented not" (Matthew 11:20). Nevertheless, with perfect submission, the Lord leaves His work with God to reward, and can say, in the day of His rejection, "Even so Father: for so it seemed good in Thy sight" (Matthew 11:26).

VERSE 5

Thirdly, if the servant of Jehovah is rejected by man, and "though Israel be not gathered", yet He will be "glorious in the eyes of the LORD". In the day of His rejection He can say of Israel, "How often *would I* have gathered thy children together … and *ye would not*" (Matthew 23:37). Nevertheless, the Servant who glorified God, and became obedient unto death, even the death of the Cross, has been highly exalted by God and given a name which is above every name and the heavens have been opened that by faith we may look up and see Jesus crowned with glory.

VERSE 6

Fourthly, during the time of Christ's rejection by the Jews – while Israel is still dispersed among the nations – Christ will be given as a light to the Gentiles, so that He may become God's salvation unto the ends of the earth.

Doubtless, the prophecy, for its complete fulfilment, looks on to the Millennial blessing of the world, but, in the meantime the Spirit of God, through the Apostle Paul, gives these beautiful words an application to the present time. When the Jews rejected the Apostle's preaching at Antioch, he uses these words as his authority for proclaiming the grace of God to the Gentiles.

Verse 7

Fifthly, as the result of Christ being proclaimed as Saviour of the world, the One who was despised of men will become the Object of worship. Jehovah is faithful to the One that men despise, and chooses the One that the nation abhors. Even the great ones of the earth will worship at His feet. This again looks on surely to a Millennial day, though even now among the Gentiles there are found those who "worship by the Spirit of God and boast in Christ Jesus" (Philippians 3:3, N.Tr.).

Verse 8

Sixthly, the day will come when the nation of Israel will be restored and brought into Millennial blessing. Being glorified by His Servant Jesus, Jehovah accepted His work, heard His cry, helped Him, and preserved Him, and *through Him*, and all that He has done, His promises to His earthly people will be fulfilled, the land will be established, and at last the nation will inherit the land that for so long has been desolate.

Verses 9-12

Then follows a touching description of the return of Israel to their land. But all is ascribed to Christ, the Servant of Jehovah. Men may seek to restore the land to the Jews, and bring them back to the land. But their efforts, even if for a time apparently successful, will only bring the Jews back for *the judgment* of the great tribulation. To come back for *blessing* they must wait until Christ gives the word. In His time He will say to the prisoners, "Go forth", and to those in darkness, "Show yourselves". Today the Jews may be exiles, oftentimes hiding from the pitiless persecution of ruthless enemies. But when Christ says "Go forth" and "Show yourselves" no power will withstand His words. No longer will they hunger and thirst nor suffer the heat of a pitiless world. For the One that has mercy upon them will Himself go before to restore His wandering sheep and lead them by springs of water and guide them over mountains and along His highways. From every quarter of the earth they will be led back.

Verse 13

Seventhly, when at last the Servant has accomplished the will of Jehovah – when the nation is restored, when the Gentiles are brought into blessing, and kings and princes shall bow and worship at His feet – then at last the heavens and the earth will join to sing His praise. The wide creation will break forth into singing and all will own that the Lord has done it all. He has comforted His people and had mercy upon His afflicted ones.

> I cannot tell how all the lands shall worship,
> When at His bidding every storm is stilled,
> Or who can say how great the jubilation
> When all the hearts of men with love are filled.
> But this I know, the skies will thrill with gladness,
> And myriad myriad human voices sing,
> And earth to heaven, and heaven to earth, will answer,
> At last the Saviour, Saviour of the world is King.[3]

---

[3] William Y. Fullerton, 1857-1932.

ISAIAH 49

VERSES 14-17

The remaining verses of the chapter speak of the faithfulness and love of Jehovah for His earthly people, set forth in the restoration of Zion, the city of God's sovereign choice (Psalm 78:68). For long centuries apparently "forsaken" and "forgotten" yet is the city loved with a compassion greater than a mother's love for a child. Her walls are continually before the Lord, and the day is coming when her children will hasten back and all her destroyers go forth from the city.

VERSES 18-21

Zion will be exalted as the nation of Israel gathers to the city. The long waste and desolate places will be found too narrow by reason of the host of the inhabitants. Astonishment will be expressed as the long hidden ones of Israel will be brought to light.

VERSES 22-23

The answer to their astonishment will be found in the realisation that the recovery of Israel is the result of the Lord lifting up His hand to the Gentiles and setting up a standard for His people. Then, indeed, the long hidden ones will come to light; they will flock to the standard of the Lord and the great ones of the earth will aid in their restoration while those who have opposed God's ancient people will lick the dust at their feet. Then it will be known that Israel's God is Jehovah – the unchanging and eternal God.

VERSES 24-26

But Israel's foes are mighty, and to mere human reason it may seem impossible that the poor down-trodden Jews will ever be delivered from the oppressor. Jehovah answers their fears with the assurance that "The captives of the mighty shall be taken away, and the prey of the terrible shall be delivered". Moreover, God will deal with those who have oppressed His people. Already the prophet has foretold that Israel, by their *restoration and blessing*, will know that the Lord God is Jehovah (verse 23); now we learn that by *judgment* the nations – all flesh – will know that Jehovah is the Saviour of Israel, their Redeemer, the mighty One of Jacob.

ISAIAH 50

In this chapter there is foretold the setting aside of the Jewish nation consequent upon their rejection of Christ, while a godly remnant is recognised, and encouraged to trust in God and obey the voice of His Servant, Jesus.

VERSE 1

The chapter opens with Jehovah reminding Israel that if they are dispersed, and in captivity to the Gentiles, and their land desolate, it is not that Jehovah has dealt lightly with them as a man might callously put away his wife, or as a heathen father might sell his child to pay his debts. It is through no lack of love on Jehovah's part that they have been set aside. Their own sins have separated them from Jehovah and brought them into captivity.

VERSES 2-3

Already the prophet has brought forward their sin in turning to idols. Now he foretells their yet greater sin in rejecting Christ. This leads the prophet, in a touching manner, to present the first coming of Christ. Looking on to the future, we hear Christ saying "I came" and "I called". But when He came there was no man to receive Him, and none to answer His call. He dwelt amongst men full of grace and truth; He spake as never man spake; He called them in words of tender love and grace. He bade the weary come unto Him and He would give them rest. But when He came to His own they received Him not, and when He called they were deaf to His entreaties.

> They closed the ear against Thy tender words,
> They chose another lord, and spurned Thy sway;
> Thou would'st have drawn them, but they snapped Thy cords;
> Thou would'st have blessed them but they turned away.[4]

But who is the One who came into the midst of Israel? The first verse commences with the words, "Thus saith Jehovah" (N.Tr.). It is Jehovah who says, "I came", and "I called". Jesus of the New Testament is the Jehovah of the Old Testament. Had, then, His hand no power to reach them in their deep need? Could He not redeem them from the enemy? Was Jehovah not the One who had all power over the heavens and the earth? In the days of old had He not put forth His power in redeeming Israel from their enemies and delivering them from Egypt? At His word the sea was dried up and "a cloud and darkness" blinded the Egyptians (Exodus 14:20-22). When in the midst of the nation in lowly grace His hand, and His word, were again seen in all their mighty power, for at His touch the leper was cleansed, the sick were healed and the dead were raised: at His word of rebuke demons were silenced and storms were stilled.

VERSE 4

But all this mighty power of Jehovah was displayed in One who "took upon Him the form of a servant, and was made in the likeness of men" (Philippians 2:7). In order that He might draw near to us in all our need He humbled Himself and became a weary, thirsty, lonely Man

---
[4] Horatius Bonar, 1808–1889, *Hymns of Faith and Hope, Second Series* (James Nisbet & Co., 1878).

to speak a word in season to a weary sinner by a well-side. To carry out this service of love, in the perfection of His Manhood He walks in perfect subjection to the Father, and takes His place morning by morning as One that is instructed to learn the Father's will. So we read of this perfect Servant, that, "In the morning, rising up a great while before day, He went out and departed into a solitary place, and there prayed" (Mark 1:35).

Verses 5-6

Thus while maintaining the glory of His Person, the prophet presents Him in all His lowliness and grace. Alas! blind to the glory of His Person, and in spite of works and words of power, men seized upon His humiliation as a reason for rejecting His claims and heaping insults upon Him. They smote Him, they plucked off the hair from His cheeks, and spat in His face. The insults of men only served to bring out the perfection of Jesus. All was met in the spirit of perfect submission. No rebellious word escaped His lips, no angry look clouded the face that man spat upon. All was met in the spirit of perfect submission that could say, "Even so, Father: for so it seemed good in Thy sight" (Luke 10:21).

Mistaken zeal may lead a disciple to draw his sword to defend His Master from the violence of men, but of the Lord we read, "Jesus ... knowing all things that should come upon Him, went forth" to meet His enemies (John 18:4). Thus He can say, "I was not rebellious, neither turned away back. I gave My back to the smiters, and My cheeks to them that plucked off the hair".

Verses 7-9

If, however, He is despised and rejected of men, if He submits to all the insults that are heaped upon Him, it was not, indeed, that He had no resource, for He can say,

"The Lord God will help Me". He may, indeed, be insulted by men, but He will not be confounded before men. So Peter can say of the Lord, when meeting the insults of men, that He "committed Himself to Him that judgeth righteously" (1 Peter 2:23). Thus looking to the Lord for help, and knowing that the Lord will justify Him from all the wicked charges that men brought against Him, He can set His face like a flint to go into death, knowing that while men may heap reproaches upon Him, yet He will not be ashamed. And if God justifies Him who will condemn? We know that the resurrection was God's answer to all the charges that men brought against Him, and all the shame they heaped upon Him. These words that are here applied to the Lord, in the New Testament, are also applied by the Spirit through the Apostle Paul to those for whom Christ died (Romans 8:33-34). If He is justified so are those for whom He died. If no charge can stand against Him, no charge will stand against those whose judgment He has borne.

In all these wondrous scenes we see the revelation of the heart of the Saviour, the exposure of the hearts of sinners, and the perfect pattern for believers. The Apostle Peter can see, in all these sufferings from the hands of men, that the Lord was leaving us an example to "follow His steps". What steps they are! To "do well", "suffer for it", and "take it patiently" (1 Peter 2:20-21).

Verse 10

Now we learn that though the nation rejects Christ there will be found in their midst a godly remnant who will fear God and listen to the voice of His Servant, Jesus. We know from the Gospel story how the presence of the Lord in the midst of Israel brought this remnant to light. He could say of them, "My sheep hear My voice, and I know them, and they follow Me" (John 10:27). They find themselves in the midst of a nation sunk in gross darkness, but the Lord could say, "I am come a light into the world, that whosoever believeth on Me should not abide in darkness" (John 12:46). So the godly soul that finds himself surrounded by spiritual darkness, and with no light for his path, is exhorted to "trust in the name of the LORD, and stay upon his God".

Man in responsibility always breaks down. As in the Jewish dispensation, so in the Christian period, the great mass becomes increasingly corrupt. But in every dispensation, however great the corruption, God preserves a remnant that fear the Lord and obey His voice. In Malachi's day there were those who feared the Lord and thought upon His Name (Malachi 3:16). In the midst of all the corruption of Christendom the Lord tells us that there will be found until the end a few, who, with little strength, will keep Christ's word and not deny His Name (Revelation 3:8), and amidst the increasing darkness we still have the Lord as our unfailing resource. However dark the day, however great our weakness, we can "be strong in the grace that is in Christ Jesus" (2 Timothy 2:1).

Thus this godly remnant is exhorted to follow in the steps of Jesus, the perfect Servant. In the presence of suffering and shame, He found in the Lord God His help (verse 7), so the godly, in the midst of a world of increasing moral darkness, can trust in the LORD and stay upon God.

VERSE 11

As for the mass of the nation, that reject the words and works of Christ, and walk in the light of their own thoughts and reasonings, they will "lie down in sorrow". The history of the Jews throughout the centuries has been a solemn witness to the greatness of that sorrow.

ISAIAH 51 to 52:12

The prophet has foretold the rejection of Christ and the consequent setting aside of the nation of Israel. He has, moreover, indicated that there will be found in their midst a remnant that fear God. In this portion he foretells the history of this remnant who in the future will form the restored nation of Israel, delivered from darkness and distress, and brought into the full glory of the day when God will reign in Zion. Their future history is foretold in a threefold appeal by Jehovah, followed by a threefold response from the remnant (verses 1, 4, 7, 9, 17, 52:1).

CHAPTER 51

VERSES 1-3

First, those that "follow after righteousness", and "seek the LORD", are exhorted to "hearken"' unto the Lord's word of comfort. They may find themselves in great weakness and few in numbers, but let them remember their father Abraham. God called him when he was *alone*; nevertheless He blessed and increased him. Zion may be forsaken, and become a wilderness and a desert, but the LORD will yet make "her wilderness like Eden, and her desert like the garden of the LORD". The present sorrows of the godly will be turned to joy and gladness, and those who "sow in tears shall reap in joy" (Psalm 126:5).

Have not the exhortations and words of comfort ministered to this godly remnant also a voice to the people of God in this day? Again we live in a day of ruin when the great Christian profession has become so utterly corrupt that it is about to be spued out of Christ's mouth. But again the word assures us that to the end there will be a few who obey Christ's word and do not deny His Name. They may find themselves with little strength and left "alone", but, as with the remnant of Israel, they are comforted with a vision of the coming glory. Paul finds himself at last in prison forsaken by all men; but the loneliness of his prison is cheered with the prospect of the glory of the heavenly Kingdom (2 Timothy 4:16-18). John finds himself in tribulation as a lonely prisoner in the Isle of Patmos for the testimony of Jesus Christ; but he is carried in spirit into heavenly scenes, there to see the glorious end of all the sufferings for Christ's sake. In that scene all tears will be wiped away, and sorrow and weeping will give place to "thanksgiving, and the voice of song" (N.Tr.).

As the outstanding characteristic of the remnant to whom Isaiah speaks is that they "follow after righteousness" (verse 1), so Scripture indicates that the first characteristic of those who separate from the corruptions of Christendom is that they "follow righteousness" (2 Timothy 2:22).

VERSES 4-6

Again the remnant are called to "hearken" unto Jehovah. Now Jehovah speaks of them as "My nation". In the day of Israel's rejection of Christ, the remnant were but a feeble few, even as Abraham, their father, in his day, was alone when called of God. In the day to come they will swell into a nation owned of God under His righteous rule. In the day of their blessing the Gentiles that have dwelt in darkness will come into the light and salvation of God, and they will trust in His arm. The heavens and the earth are a witness to the everlasting character of God's salvation founded upon His righteousness.

Verses 7-8

For the third time the godly remnant are called to hearken. They have been comforted, in their loneliness and weakness, with the vision of the coming glory. Now, in the light of that glory, they are strengthened to face "the reproach of men", and the "revilings", that will ever be the portion of those who, in a day of ruin, fear the Lord, obey His voice and "follow after righteousness" (verse 1). Thus, those in our day who, in obedience to the word separate themselves from the corruptions of Christendom will meet with reproach, for the word to such is, "Let us go forth therefore unto Him without the camp, bearing His reproach" (Hebrews 13:13). However, the godly, in any day of ruin, need not fear the reproaches and revilings of those of whom God says they will pass away like a moth-eaten garment.

In answer to this threefold appeal we have the threefold response of the godly, commencing with the words, "Awake, awake" (verses 9, 17, 52:1).

Verses 9-10

First, in view of their future blessing, the godly, led by the Spirit, call for the power of the Lord to be put forth "as in the ancient days" when Jehovah delivered the nation from Egypt, and dried up the Red Sea making a way for "the ransomed to pass over".

Verse 11

Having hearkened to the LORD's promise of future blessing, and with the assurance of God's power in the past, the remnant can say with confidence, "The redeemed of the LORD shall return, and come with singing unto Zion". And when they return "everlasting joy shall be upon their head: they shall obtain gladness and joy; and sorrow and mourning shall flee away".

Verses 12-16

In response to this appeal, Jehovah comforts the remnant, and exhorts them not to fear man or "the fury of the oppressor". Man is but as grass that perishes; Jehovah that comforts them is the Maker of the heavens and the earth. Therefore His captive exiles will be set free: His starving people will be fed. He can still the waves that roar: He can make His people a testimony by putting His words into their mouths. He can protect His people; plant them in the land and say of them, "Thou art *My* people". So of the overcomer in this day of ruin – the one that keeps His word and does not deny His name – the Lord can say that in the day of glory "I will write upon him the name of *My* God, the name of the city of *My* God ... and I will write upon him *My* new name" (Revelation 3:12).

Verses 17-23

Secondly, having the LORD's promise to restore Zion, the godly remnant appeal to Jerusalem to awake from her long slumber. The city had indeed suffered for her sins, and above all for its rejection of Christ, and thus drunk of the cup of the fury of the LORD. With no one among her own children to guide, her position for generations has been one of desolation, destruction, the famine and the sword. Now the prophet looks on to the day when her sorrows will be over, and the cup of judgment will be taken from her lips and become the portion of those who have afflicted her and trodden her under foot.

CHAPTER 52

Verses 1-6

In view of this promised deliverance, the godly remnant, for the third time, appeal to Zion to "awake" and come forth in all her glory, and shine in the beauty of holiness. No more will the unclean nations besiege the city. Never again will Egypt or Assyria – the southern and northern nations – oppress the city without cause, making God's people howl with misery and blaspheming God's Name.

Verses 7-8

The good news will be sounded abroad. It will be said of Zion, "Thy God reigneth". Then at last when the Nation is restored, Israel and Judah will sing together, for they shall see eye to eye. But all this blessing will be wholly the work of the Lord, for it will be "when the Lord shall bring again Zion".

Verses 9-10

Then we learn that when at last the restored nation breaks into singing, the great theme of their song will be the Lord, and what He has done. "The Lord hath comforted His people"; "He hath redeemed Jerusalem", and "The Lord hath made bare His holy arm in the eyes of all the nations". And may we not say that the time is coming when it will be true of His scattered people of today, who so often have fallen out by the way, that "with the voice together shall they sing", and that will be when at last "they shall see eye to eye" (verse 8). And shall we not see eye to eye when at last we see Christ face to face. And even now, if we were each looking to Christ, should we not see eye to eye and "be of the same mind in the

Lord"? (Philippians 4:2). Seeing eye to eye we shall break into singing, and He will be the great theme of our song. With all the redeemed we shall sing the new song, "Thou art worthy ... for Thou wast slain, and hast redeemed us to God by Thy blood ... and hast made us unto our God kings and priests" (Revelation 5:9-10).

Verses 11-12

Finally, in view of this great deliverance Jehovah's people are exhorted to separate from the unclean of the nations, for those that bear the vessels of the LORD must be clean. Their deliverance from the nations will be no hasty flight, for the LORD will surround their going. He will go before to lead the way, and He will be their rereward for their protection.

ISAIAH 52:13 to 53:12

In chapters 49 to 52:12, we have seen Christ presented as the Servant of Jehovah coming into the world in humiliation to fulfil the counsels of God. In His humiliation He is rejected by the nation of Israel, but received by the God-fearing remnant who obey the voice of Jehovah's Servant (50:10).

In this fresh division, commencing with verse 13 of chapter 52, we have, in the first place, Christ as the Servant of Jehovah, presented in His exaltation. Again He is rejected by the nation, but owned by a repentant remnant, who, having confessed their sin and the sin of the nation, learn that their blessing, and the pleasure of the LORD, is secured by the atoning sufferings of Christ.

CHAPTER 52
Verses 13-15

This portion of the prophecy opens with foretelling the exaltation of Christ – the Servant of Jehovah. "He shall be exalted and be lifted up, and be very high" (N.Tr.). So it came to pass, when the nation had rejected their Messiah presented to them in lowly grace on earth, a further and final testimony to Christ in exaltation was rendered to that generation. Thus we hear the Apostles announce that "This Jesus hath God raised up", and they add, "Let all the house of Israel know assuredly, that God hath made that same Jesus, whom ye have crucified, both Lord and Christ" (Acts 2:32-36).

Moreover, the prophet foretells that as many had been astonished who saw Him in humiliation, when "His visage was so marred more than any man, and His form more than the sons of men", so will many be "astonished" (N.Tr.) when they see the One that was nailed to a cross, crowned with glory on a throne. The prophet would seem to carry us on to the full results of Christ's exaltation in Millennial days when the great ones of the earth will at last see, and hear, that which faith already anticipates. In His humiliation, "the kings of the earth set themselves, and the rulers take counsel together, against the LORD, and against His Anointed, saying, Let us break their bands asunder, and cast away their cords from us" (Psalm 2:2-3). But the time is coming when every mouth will be shut, and every knee will bow before the King of Kings and the Lord of Lords.

CHAPTER 53

Verse 1

Even as the nation rejected both the words and works of Christ in humiliation, so, too, they reject the mighty "arm of the LORD" manifested in raising Christ from the dead and exalting Him in glory, as well as the "report" of His glory rendered by the Holy Spirit through the Apostles.

Verses 2-6

If, however, the testimony to an exalted Christ is rejected by the mass of the nation we learn that again there will be a repentant remnant who will be convicted of their sin by the report of the exaltation of the One that they had crucified. In these verses we hear the confession of this remnant. It takes a threefold character:–

- First, they own that in the day of His humiliation they had despised and rejected their Messiah. They see now that under the eye of God He was altogether lovely – a tender plant. At last in this barren world there was a "root" that would bring forth fruit for God. But the remnant own that they form part of a nation of whom they have to say, "When we saw Him, there is no beauty that we should desire Him". Man may wonder at His words of wisdom, and His mighty works but they despised and rejected Him because of His lowly grace. They esteemed Him of no importance as they say, "Is not this the carpenter's son?" (Matthew 13:54-58).

- Secondly, by faith they now see that if He was the Man of sorrows, it was because He was bearing their griefs and carrying their sorrows, and if, on the cross, He was stricken, smitten, and afflicted, it was for their sins He was wounded and bruised, that through His atoning sufferings they might have peace and healing.

- Thirdly, in the light of the cross, and realising the mighty efficacy of that work, they can fully own their sin. They can say, "All we like sheep have gone astray; we have turned every one to his own way". Nevertheless, they see that all their sins have been righteously dealt with, for they can say, "The LORD hath laid on Him the iniquity of us all".

VERSES 7-9

We have listened to the confession of the godly remnant; now we are to hear the voice of Jehovah as He confirms their confession and bears witness to the excellencies of

ISAIAH 52:13 TO 53:12

Christ. Already the remnant have confessed that He was stricken and afflicted; now Jehovah bears witness to His perfection, inasmuch that when He was afflicted and oppressed "He opened not His mouth", and "as a sheep before her shearers is dumb, so He openeth not His mouth". Men may oppress and afflict, but, if He was stricken, it was not for any wrong doing on His part, for "He had done no violence, neither was any deceit in His mouth". He submitted to every indignity from man in order to carry out the will of God in bearing the transgression of God's people.

In after years we see how the Spirit of God uses the Apostle Peter to apply the prophet's words to the believing remnant of the scattered nation of Israel. If the prophet says "All we like sheep have gone astray", the Apostle can write of the remnant, "Ye were as sheep going astray". If the prophet can say of Christ, "He had done no violence, neither was any deceit in His mouth", so the Apostle can say, "He did no sin, neither was guile found in His mouth". If the prophet foretells that in the presence of insults "He opened not His mouth", so the Apostle can say He was One who "when He was reviled, reviled not again; when He suffered He threatened not". If Jehovah can say by the prophet, "For the transgression of My people was He stricken", so the Apostle can say, "Who His own self bare our sins in His own body on the tree" (1 Peter 2:21-25).

The Apostle tells us that if the Lord was silent in the presence of the insults that men heaped upon Him, it was not that He was without resource. Instead of answering the false charges of men, He committed Himself to God that judgeth righteously. It is clear that the wickedness of men was only carrying out the counsels that God had determined before to be done (Acts 2:23, 4:27-28). But that will being accomplished, God will allow no further indignities to be heaped upon His holy Servant, Jesus; though "men appointed His grave with the wicked" (N.Tr.) yet God decreed that He was with the rich in His death (John 19:38-42).

VERSE 10

Again the remnant bear their witness to the sufferings of Christ. They have owned man's part in rejecting and delivering Christ to be crucified; now they look beyond all the wickedness of man, and they see that Christ suffered at the hands of a holy God when His soul was made an offering for sin.

They see that the LORD has bruised Him and put Him to grief. The wickedness of man in crucifying Christ brings judgment upon man. His death viewed as that by which He would accomplish the will of God, brings glory to God and blessing to man. Thus the remnant can say, "When *Thou* shalt make His soul an offering for sin, He shall see His seed, He shall prolong His days, and the pleasure of the LORD shall prosper in His hand". Death, that for us would cut off all hope of a seed, would end our days, and blight all our prospects, becomes, for the Lord, the way by which He secures a seed, whereby He enters into an endless risen life beyond the power of death, and above all, the way whereby the pleasure of the LORD can prosper.

Thus there pass before us three great results that flow from the death of Christ accomplishing the will of God:–

- First, through His offering, there is secured the vast host of the redeemed – His seed – even as the Lord can say to His disciples "Except a corn of wheat fall into the ground and die, it abideth alone: but if it die, it bringeth forth much fruit" (John 12:24).

- Secondly, "He shall prolong His days". So in the Psalms we read, "He asked life of Thee, and Thou gavest it Him, even length of days for ever and ever" (Psalm 21:4). But that life is a risen life, that no power of death can touch, and no power of the enemy can take from the believer, for the Lord can say of His sheep, "I give unto them eternal life; and they shall never perish, neither shall any one pluck them out of My hand" (John 10:28).

- Thirdly, as the result of His death the pleasure of the LORD prospers in His hand. In each successive age man has entirely failed to carry out the will of God. Set in responsibility we have always broken down. Nevertheless, the pleasure of the LORD will not be thwarted, for at last in the hands of the risen Christ it will prosper.

VERSES 11-12

Again we hear Jehovah speaking as He confirms the word of the remnant, and bears witness to his righteous Servant. The remnant had said, "He shall see His seed"; now Jehovah says "He shall see of the fruit of the travail of His soul, and shall be satisfied" (N.Tr.). These are words that include not only the redeemed of Israel, but that great host that will be with Him and like Him in heavenly glory. And the believer can say, "I shall be satisfied, when I awake, with Thy likeness" (Psalm 17:15). Thus we learn that it is the pleasure of the LORD that there shall be a vast host of redeemed, made like to Christ, as the fruit of His work, and for the joy of His heart. All this will be the result of the work of Jehovah's "righteous Servant", One who could say, "Lo, I come to do Thy will, O God" (Psalm 40:7-8; Hebrews 10:7). By His work He justifies those who are brought to know Him, by bearing their iniquities.

Moreover, the One that does this great work is exalted, while the great enemy of God and man, is defeated and robbed of his spoil.

Thus we learn that through the atoning death of Christ:–

(1) A great company of redeemed is secured – His seed;

(2) A life beyond the power of death is entered upon;

(3) The pleasure of the LORD prospers;

(4) The heart of Christ is satisfied with the fruit of His work;

(5) Believers are justified;

(6) Christ is exalted;

(7) The enemy is defeated.

All this blessing is traced up to the wonderful fact that Christ, in His perfect obedience to the Father's will, "Poured out His soul unto death". The remnant have already seen God acting in delivering Christ to death, when Jehovah made His soul an offering for sin; now they see that Jehovah delights to exalt Christ – to "assign Him a portion with the great" (N.Tr.).

Thus, in this great passage, we see the death of Christ presented in a threefold aspect. First, as brought about by the wickedness of men; secondly, as the act of God Who delivered Him up, and put Him to grief; thirdly, as the act of Christ, Himself, when, in obedience to the will of God, He "poured out His soul unto death".

ISAIAH 54

VERSES 1-6

In chapter 53 we hear the Spirit of God foretelling the sufferings of Christ and the glories that will follow. In chapter 54 we learn that, following upon the exaltation of Christ, there will be a future restoration of the Jewish nation that in the days that are past had enjoyed a place of nearness to Jehovah, set forth by the figure of the marriage-tie. Alas! they had been faithless to Jehovah, broken His law, turned to idols, and rejected their Messiah. Thus, Jerusalem, and her cities, had become desolate, and, like a faithless wife, that has been refused, Jehovah had forsaken the nation in His wrath, and hidden His face from them.

Nevertheless, as we have seen, a remnant will be brought to repentance, and on the ground of the sufferings of Christ, will come into blessing and form the restored nation that will outnumber the Jews during the time of their desolation. In meeting this increase the restored nation is called to rejoice and enlarge her borders. Moreover, it is foretold, that, the people of Jerusalem will inherit the seed of the Gentiles; for their God is the

Redeemer, the Holy One of Israel, Who will be owned as "the God of the whole earth".

Verses 7-10

Moreover, if God had forsaken the nation in His wrath, it will be with "great mercies" and "everlasting kindness" that He will regather them, and when restored it will be for everlasting blessing. Even as God has sworn that the waters of Noah should no more go over the earth, so He will no more be wrath with Israel. The mountains, that look so immovable may depart, and the hills be removed, but the kindness of God will not depart from the nation.

Verses 11-14

The prophet then uses the figure of precious stones to set forth the moral beauty that will shine forth from restored Israel. The nation will be taught of the LORD, and great will be their peace, for they will be established in righteousness. No longer will they be oppressed, nor live in fear and terror.

Verses 15-17

There may be those who will gather together against the nation, but no longer, in the government of God, will such be allowed to triumph over His People. On the contrary, their opposition to God's people will bring about their own downfall, for God has prepared instruments for dealing in judgment with the opposers. No weapon formed against the servants of the LORD will prosper. Every tongue that speaks against them will be silenced in judgment.

ISAIAH 55

If God, in the restoration of Israel, acts "with great mercies" as foretold in the previous chapter (verse 7), what is to hinder the same grace flowing out to a needy and sinful world! Thus, in chapter 55, we have the invitation of free grace proclaimed to "every one" – Jew and Gentile alike.

Verses 1-3

In the first three verses we hear the voice of Jehovah appealing in sovereign grace to needy Israel. Those in soul need, with no resources to meet their need, can have the blessing in pure grace. Why then labour to obtain blessing by their own efforts, only to find that no works of man can satisfy the longing of the soul? Let all such cease from their own doings and "hearken diligently" to God's invitation in grace, and thus enter into and enjoy the fulness of blessing that grace provides.

Those that listen and come to God, will "live", and thus enter into the everlasting blessings promised to David. By the "everlasting covenant" David was assured that, through his seed, God would establish his kingdom and throne for ever (see 2 Samuel 7:12-17, Psalm 89:34-37, Jeremiah 33:19-32). We know from Acts 13 verse 34, that the Spirit of God clearly indicates that Christ is the promised seed of David, and that the sure mercies of David are secured through Christ risen from the dead. Thus the grace of God flows out to Jew and Gentile in righteousness on the firm foundation of the death and resurrection of Christ.

VERSE 4

At once Jehovah appeals to the Gentiles (or "peoples", N.Tr.) through Christ. He is given as a witness to the grace of God to the whole world, and as Prince and Commander of the nations.

VERSE 5

Having appealed to Israel and the nations, God now addresses Christ, announcing that there will be an answer to His proclamation of grace that will gather the nations to the One that God has glorified. Thus we have a threefold witness to the grace of God – grace to Israel secured by Christ risen, grace proclaimed through Christ to the nations, and grace drawing the nations to Christ glorified.

VERSES 6-7

Seeing there is grace for all, an appeal is made to men to seek the Lord in a day of grace – "while He may be found", and to call "upon Him while He is near". Men may have their "way", and their "thoughts", as to the way of obtaining blessing. But the wicked man is urged to "forsake his way" and "his thoughts" and return to the LORD to receive abundance of blessing on the ground of grace.

ISAIAH 55

Verses 8-11

God's thoughts and God's ways are far above man's legal thoughts and ways, even as the heavens are higher than the earth. God's blessing, like the rain, comes down from heaven; as with the rain, so with His word, it accomplishes the end for which it is sent.

Verses 12-13

His sowing of the good seed of His word of grace will bring forth a harvest of "joy" and "peace", hush creation's groan, secure blessing for man, and the everlasting glory of the name of the Lord.

ISAIAH 56 and 57

In the closing portion of this division of the prophecy – we have first, in verses 1 to 8, encouragement for the godly in view of the Millennial blessing that is "near to come"; secondly, from verse 9 of chapter 56 to the end of chapter 57, warnings to the ungodly mass of the nation, closing with a contrast between the contrite remnant and the restless wicked.

CHAPTER 56

Verse 1

Encouragement for the godly. In the preceding chapter we have heard the call of grace to every needy soul to seek the Lord while He may be found, with the promise of blessing to all that respond to the call. In the opening verses of this chapter, the godly remnant in Israel, who have responded to the call, are exhorted to walk in consistency with the grace that has blessed them. Let such act righteously having in view God's salvation for the nation of Israel that is "near to come", and the righteousness of God in judgment upon the wicked, which is about to be revealed.

ISAIAH 56 AND 57

Verse 2

The godly man that observes the Sabbath and "keepeth his hand from doing any evil" will be blessed. The mention of the Sabbath clearly shows that, as in the previous chapter, the prophecy has in view the blessing of the Jewish nation in latter days.

Verses 3-8

These verses that specially speak of the stranger and the hopeless – the eunuch – clearly show that the earthly blessings of God's salvation will not be confined to the godly remnant of Israel. Such need not view themselves as shut out from blessing, by saying, "The LORD hath utterly separated me from His people"; for if there are those among the nations that fear the LORD, by keeping His sabbaths and choosing the things that please the LORD, and avail themselves of the promise of blessing on the ground of grace, they, too, will have a portion in God's house, and come into the everlasting blessing and joy of God's earthly people. For God's house will be called "an house of prayer for all nations". Not only will the outcasts of Israel be brought back to their land, but others from among the Gentiles will be gathered to God's earthly centre of blessing.

Verse 9

Warnings to the ungodly. These warnings open with a solemn picture of the Gentile world. As in the prophecy of Daniel, the great Gentile empires are likened to beasts that act without any fear of God, so in this prophecy they are viewed as preying upon the nation of Israel. How solemnly is this scripture being fulfilled today, when so-called Christian nations are ruthlessly seeking the destruction of the Jews.[5]

---

[5] The situation when the author was writing in 1941.

Verses 10-12

But what of the Jewish leadership? In the verses that follow we see a solemn portrayal of their spiritual condition in the sight of God. Having rejected Christ, their leaders are *"blind" to their own condition* and *"ignorant" of the grace of God.* Like "dumb dogs" they "cannot bark" (N.Tr.) and so are *unable to warn others.* Like sleeping dogs they love to slumber, and thus *seek their present ease.* Like greedy dogs, they *seek their own gain.* They live only for the present and *have no thought for the future.* What a solemn picture!

CHAPTER 57

Verses 1-2

Thus the righteous remnant among God's people may perish but "no man layeth it to heart". Nevertheless if the godly are taken away it is a solemn sign that judgment is about to fall, for "the righteous is taken away from the evil to come". So has it ever been in the history of the world. As one has said: "When Lots are taken out of Sodom, it presages a shower of wrath. Methuselah was taken away a year before the flood. ... We may conclude that when Noahs are taken into their arks, it betokens a deluge, and that God gathers His harvest before the winter storm, and calls home labourers before the dark night comes on."[6]

Verses 3-4

Then follows a solemn picture of the condition of the apostate Jews in the last days. Having rejected their Messiah they fall into idolatry and turn to Anti-christ. In view of the coming judgments that will fall upon the nation, the Jews are invited to "draw near" and heed God's

---

[6] R. Erskine, 1685-1752, *Sermons and Other Practical Works*, Volume II, 1821.

warnings, for it is ever God's way to warn men before He acts in judgment. When Christ came into the midst of the nation it was no longer marked by idolatry, as in the days of the kings, but having rejected Christ, they are warned by the Lord that the unclean spirit of idolatry would enter into their midst in a more terrible form than in the days of old; so that their last state will be worse than their first (Luke 11:24-26). The prophet looks on to these solemn days. He sees that, having rejected Christ, they proved themselves to be the sons of the sorceress – the offspring of those in league with the devil, even as the Lord can say, "Ye are of your father the devil" (John 8:44), the seed of those who have been unfaithful to Jehovah.

Jehovah addresses to such two searching questions, "Against whom do ye sport yourselves? against whom make ye a wide mouth, and draw out the tongue?" We hear the Lord's own answer to these questions in Psalm 35, "In Mine adversity they rejoiced … with hypocritical mockers … they gnashed upon *Me* with their teeth" … "they opened their mouth wide against *Me*". Rejecting Christ and His word, they believe a lie, and instead of forming part of His seed (Isaiah 53:10), they become "a seed of falsehood".

Verses 5-9

The result of believing a lie is seen in the gross idolatry and superstition into which the nation will fall. They inflame themselves with idols, offer up their children, and worship stones. Will such offerings be any comfort to the Lord? Upon the high hills, and behind the doors of the temple they set up their idols to whom they turn rather than to Jehovah. Above all, they will turn to the false king – to Anti-christ. This, surely, is the one to whom the Lord referred when He said to the Jews, "I am come in My

Father's name, and ye receive Me not: if another shall come in his own name, him ye will receive" (John 5:43). Daniel describes this wicked king as doing according to his own will, exalting himself above every god, and speaking against the God of gods (Daniel 11:36-40). In turning to this king the nation will debase itself to hell (verse 9).

VERSES 10-12

Wearied with the multitude of their ways, the nation will say there is no hope, and so turn to the false king to find a passing quickening of their strength (N.Tr.). In turning to the false king they forget Jehovah their true resource in time of trouble. Their lack of all fear of God shows that their heart is untouched and their conscience unreached. They may boast in their own righteousness and words, but these will not profit them.

VERSES 13-21

This warning word closes with a striking contrast between the guilty nation and the godly remnant. The nation may cry out in distress only to find that those in whom they have put their trust will be carried away by a breath of wind. In contrast we are reminded of the godly remnant who put their trust in Jehovah. They will possess the Land, a way will be cast up for their return to God's earthly centre, and every stumbling-block will be taken out of their path. The One that inhabiteth eternity can stoop to revive a contrite and humble soul of earth, even as "the only-begotten Son, who is in the bosom of the Father," "became flesh, and dwelt among us … full of grace and truth" (John 1:18, 14). The result will be that, after judgment has done its work, God will lead the godly back into their Land, bless them with comforts, and bring peace, not only to the godly remnant – those that are "near" – but to the Gentile that is "afar off" (verse 19). But the wicked are like the troubled sea when it cannot rest. For such, there is "no peace".

Other Books by Hamilton Smith from Scripture Truth Publications

"The Lord is My Shepherd" and Other Papers
> ISBN 978-0-901860-06-4; (paperback)
> 97 pages; July 1987

UNDERSTANDING THE NEW TESTAMENT Series

The Gospel of Mark: An Expository Outline
> ISBN 978-0-901860-69-9; (paperback)
> ISBN 978-0-901860-70-5; (hardback)
> 144 pages; March 2007

The Epistle to the Romans: An Expository Outline
> ISBN 978-0-901860-85-9; (paperback)
> 196 pages; June 2008

The Epistle to the Colossians: An Expository Outline
> ISBN 978-0-901860-90-3; (paperback)
> 68 pages; June 2009

UNDERSTANDING THE OLD TESTAMENT Series

Elijah: A Prophet of the Lord
> ISBN 978-0-901860-68-2; (paperback)
> 80 pages; March 2007

Elisha: The Man of God
> ISBN 978-0-901860-79-8; (paperback)
> 92 pages; March 2007

UNDERSTANDING CHRISTIANITY Series

Short Papers on the Church
> ISBN 978-0-901860-80-4; (paperback)
> 96 pages; March 2008

GOD, ISRAEL, IDOLATRY AND CHRIST

GLEANINGS FROM THE PAST SERIES

EXTRACTS FROM THE LETTERS OF SAMUEL RUTHERFORD
 ISBN 978-0-901860-81-1; (paperback)
 96 pages; March 2008

EXTRACTS FROM THE WRITINGS OF WILLIAM GURNALL
 ISBN 978-0-901860-82-8; (paperback)
 100 pages; August 2008

EXTRACTS FROM THE WRITINGS OF THOMAS WATSON
 ISBN 978-0-901860-83-5; (paperback)
 96 pages; April 2009

www.ingramcontent.com/pod-product-compliance
Lightning Source LLC
Chambersburg PA
CBHW061340040426

42444CB000011B/3019